BASIC ✳ ESSENTIALS™
SNOWBOARDING

Help Us Keep This Guide Up to Date

Every effort has been made by the author and editors to make this guide as accurate and useful as possible. However, many things can change after a guide is published—organizations close, phone numbers change, companies come under new management, etc.

We would love to hear from you concerning your experiences with this sourcebook and how you feel it could be made better and be kept up to date. While we may not be able to respond to all comments and suggestions, we'll take them to heart and we'll also make certain to share them with the author. Please send your comments and suggestions to the following address:

The Globe Pequot Press
Reader Response/Editorial Department
P.O. Box 480
Guilford, CT 06437

Or you may e-mail us at:

editorial@globe-pequot.com

Thanks for your input.

BASIC ✶ ESSENTIALS™
SNOWBOARDING

SECOND EDITION

JOHN MCMULLEN

ILLUSTRATIONS BY THE AUTHOR

The
Globe
Pequot
Press

Guilford, Connecticut

Cover design by Lana Mullen
Cover photo © Photodisc, Inc.
Text design by Casey Shain
Text photographs courtesy of Burton Snowboards (pp. 3, 21), John McMullen (pp. 27, 28, 29, 30, 31), and Sunday River Resort/Sharon McNeill (pp. 4, 47, 60)

Basic Essentials is a trademark of The Globe Pequot Press.

Library of Congress Cataloging-in-Publication Data.
McMullen, John, 1958–
    Basic essentials: Snowboarding / John McMullen : illustrations by the author. — 2nd ed.
        p.   cm. — (Basic essentials series)
    Rev. ed. of: The basic essentials of snowboarding. 1991.
    Includes index.
    ISBN 0-7627-0523-X
    1. Snowboarding. I. McMullen, John, 1958– Basic essentials of snowboarding. II. Title III. Title: Snowboarding.
GV857.S57M37   1999
796.9—dc21
                                                                    00-44353
                                                                    CIP

Manufactured in the United States of America
Second Edition/First Printing

Contents

Dedication

This book is dedicated to my mother, who always told me I could do anything if I put my mind to it, and to my wife Cathy Carlisle-McMullen for her help and support while I worked through all our weekends together.

Acknowledgments

I would like to thank my high school art teachers Mr. Downey and Mr. Ken Piene for their guidance, and Bonnie and Jim for turning me on to the sport of snowboarding.

Introduction

As I stand on the edge of the ridge, the view of the mountains bathed in an alpine glow is spectacular. A gust of wind blows a wave of snow up and over the corniced edge. Looking down, I feel the depths of the couloir pulling me. My heart pounds with the surge of adrenaline.

An invigorating day of climbing steep sections of ice and rock has brought me to the top of the run, a gorge cutting into the face of the mountain. Today the conditions are good. In summer this couloir is only 5 feet wide in some places, but now it is filled with solid, stable snow.

I plan to descend this route on a snowboard. My concentration and balance must be perfect. A fall would send me a thousand feet or more down the mountain. Visualizing the turns and jumps, I picture the perfect, flawless run.

My partner and I pull out our radio transceivers and check their operation. If one of us should get caught in an avalanche, the radio signal may be our only chance for survival.

I slip my snowboard out of the pack. It's a modern sled, made solely for the purpose of going down hills fast. I step into the front binding, clipping it securely to my boot. Carefully, I slide to the edge of the abyss. Sitting on the edge, I fit the back binding to my boot. Looking down the couloir, I can see my line. It's time to ride.

I raise my arms and tip the nose of my board over the edge. The slope is steep, the snow hard and fast. Rock flashes in front of my face. Centering myself and compressing, I lean forward into a frontside turn to slow my speed. I ride up onto a wall of snow, lean back on my heels, and swing my front arm back over the nose of the board. The snow flies from the bottom of my board in a feathery rooster tail as I cut the turn.

Carving short turns to control my speed, I work my way down the seemingly endless pipe. Suddenly I see a rise in front of me. I hit the crest of it and find myself completely airborne. Keeping my weight forward and my arms up to maintain balance, I fly through the air. The powder below catches me and spits me out.

Ahead of me the run opens up. I see a wind-sculpted cornice formed on a ridge and head for it. Setting up to hit the face of it, I gain speed and race up the wall. It's steep and I slow down, but not before I leave the top. In the air I twist, planting my hand on the lip, and turn to slide back down the face. Leaning back on my board, I float through the steep powder.

My partner catches up with me as we hit the tree line. We carve turns through groves of aspen, pine, and spruce. Between the shadows, the sun reflects off the snow like millions of tiny mirrors. It has been another beautiful day of boarding.

I often wonder if the inventor of the snowboard ever imagined that the sport would develop into what it is today: the extreme descents, the radical maneuvers in the halfpipe, and the speed now attainable in the slalom and downhill.

History and Development of the Snowboard

From Snurfer to Snowboard

Jem made the first "snowboard" in the late 1960s. It was called the Snurfer, for snow surfer. The Snurfer was larger than a skateboard, with a slightly upturned nose to which a rope was attached. The surface of the board was covered with staples to give your boots better grip. These Snurfer boards were difficult to control, but fun to ride.

It took many years before the snowboard saw much change in design. In 1979 Jake Burton Carpenter showed up at a contest with a new board he had designed. The Burton board was longer and wider than the Snurfer and had the addition of bungee boot bindings. These bindings were set at an angle compared to the stance used on a skateboard. This allowed faster rides and tricks to be performed with more control. Within a couple of years, bindings were standard equipment on all snowboards.

New board and binding designs soon followed. One of these new designs was the Winterstick. This board had many design features that made it popular. Bigger than the Snurfer board, it had a radical shape that allowed better turning control as well as a wide nose that enabled it to float easily over deep powder snow.

Today many ski manufacturers and independent designers are making snowboards. New developments in surface materials, core materials, and board shapes are being made every day.

Snowboard Styles

Snowboards come in a wide variety of shapes and sizes, each suitable for a particular style of riding. There are boards configured for the three basic styles of riding—freestyle, freeriding, and freecarving. Each style requires some special design features.

♦ Freestyle boards made for freestyle snowboarding have twin tips and soft flex patterns. They're designed for trick riding and halfpipe riding. This is a good board design for beginners to use.

♦ Freeriding boards have a twin-tip design and soft to stiff flex pattern. They're general-purpose boards made for all types of riding. Backcountry riders prefer this type of board. Freeride boards with soft flex patterns are good for beginners.

♦ Freecarving boards have a single-tip design, little or no tail kick, and a stiff flex pattern. They're slim and long and made for carving turns on steep, smooth runs. A more specialized version of this type of board, the slalom board, has an asymmetrical sidecut. It is designed specifically for downhill racing. This type of board is not recommended for beginners.

The latest snowboard designs include radical sidecut radii for improved turn control and a wide variety of flex patterns.

Another piece of equipment that has seen significant development is the snowboarding boot. Many manufacturers these days are making boots specially designed for snowboarding. The new designs feature heavy-duty construction and high tops for more support to the ankle and lower leg. Soft snowboarding boots are made of leather and plastics. This type of boot is made to be used with strap-on bindings.

Step-in bindings require special boots constructed to give more support than those made for strap-in bindings. Step-in boots may or may not have internal highback inserts to stiffen the back of the boot for more support. Some step-in bindings are made with highbacks, making it possible to wear a more comfortable, softer boot with them. Remember, if you're thinking of getting a step-in binding system, make sure the boot fits first. You can get the coolest bindings going, but if the boot doesn't fit you'll be miserable on the hill.

Another boot choice is the hard boot. Hard snowboarding boots are very similar to alpine ski boots but more flexible. The boot consists of an outer shell usually made of plastic, and an inner boot or boot liner constructed from insulating material. To use this type of boot, you need a plate binding. The bails on the front and back of the binding attach to the front and back welts of the hard boot's shell.

Figure 1-1

Snowboards come in a variety of shapes, sizes, and colors.

Hard boots have an insulated inner boot that makes them very warm. This type of boot offers an incredible amount of turning and edge control. They are the choice of most freecarving, slalom, and extreme backcountry riders.

Snowboarding Competition

Competitive snowboarding started soon after the first snowboards were made. Originally, these events were put on mostly for fun; they gave the few riders who were around the chance to see each other's tricks and to learn new ones.

With the improvements in snowboarding equipment, the number of riders grew. In order to advertise their snowboarding-related products and services, ski resorts, manufacturers, and clothing companies began to sponsor competitions and riders. Presently, snowboarding competitions are held at many ski resorts. Riders can compete in freestyle, slalom, downhill, boardercross, halfpipe, and extreme events. There are competitions for both men and women, and often there are categories especially for younger and older riders.

In freestyle competition a snowboarder is judged on the creativity and difficulty of the tricks performed. This type of competition is held on a mogul run with lots of bumps and jumps. A variation on freestyle competition is the "big air" event, held on a short run with

one or more big jumps. Riders go for it, doing all sorts of tricks, spins, and flips. It's a fun event to watch.

Snowboarders also compete in slalom races. Speed and accuracy are the crucial elements of this type of event. The downhill is the traditional race. It's held on a long, steep, smooth course, and the rider with the fastest time wins.

Boardercross is the latest rage in snowboard riding and competition. Each rider competes against several others on one course, which is designed with numerous jumps and turns, plus straight sections where speed is essential. It's a dash to the finish line and the fastest racer is the winner. This type of competition also gets an A-plus for spectator enjoyment.

Halfpipe competitions are very dynamic. Usually man-made, a competition halfpipe is shaped like a pipe that's cut in half lengthwise and slightly tilted to one end. The rider drops into the pipe on the upper end and performs tricks off the walls. Expert riders often fly up into the air to perform their tricks—very exciting to watch. Riders are judged on their creativity and the difficulty of the tricks.

Extreme snowboarding competitions are held on very steep, very rocky terrain. They're dangerous enough to make even the hardest-core snowboarders' palms sweat. This type of competition requires skills in route finding, snow conditions, and extreme control during every move down the mountain.

You can snowboard at almost any ski resort. By buying a regular pass, you can take a lift to the top of the best hills in the world, ride in some fantastic pipes, or enjoy some specialized snowboard parks. Snowboarding at resorts is great fun. Runs of all levels of difficulty are available for boarders ranging from beginner to expert. There are only a few resorts left in the country that don't allow snowboarders; if you have any doubts, call before you go.

Backcountry Snowboarding

Backcountry snowboarding is very popular. This type of snowboarding takes place in undeveloped mountainous areas where you must take a Snowcat ride, ski, hike, and sometimes climb to get to the top of the desired run. The most remote areas are only accessible by helicopter or Snowcat.

Snowboarding in the backcountry requires extensive knowledge of wilderness survival skills. Understanding weather and snow conditions, having the correct gear, and knowing how to use it are essential. From Alaska to Patagonia, from the Matterhorn to Mount Kilimanjaro, you'll find serious descents down the steepest, highest mountains in the world. Snowboarders have climbed mountains and made descents that would make your hair stand on end.

How to Pick a Snowboard

The sport of snowboarding requires very little equipment. A snowboard, snowboarding boots, eye protection, and warm clothing are about all you will need.

The foundation of this equipment is, of course, the snowboard. A close relative of the snow ski, the snowboard is constructed in much the same way, but is wider to accommodate a sideways stance (similar to a skateboard or surfboard) on the board. The variety of snowboards is endless. Manufacturers make boards designed for specific styles of riding—freestyle, freeriding, freecarving, and slalom—in many lengths and widths.

Choose Your Stance

If you've ever been on a skateboard or surfboard, you'll know what direction to face when you set up your snowboard. If you face right while on a board you have what's called a "normal" stance. If you face left, you have a "goofy" stance. If you're unsure what your stance is, just start with a normal setup. You'll know if it is right or wrong for you pretty quickly once you get up on the board.

Your stance may or may not have a bearing on choosing your ride. If you'll be getting a board with sidecuts that are asymmetrical, you'll need to know your stance preference before you make the purchase. Otherwise, though, most boards are made with symmetrical sidecuts. Your stance won't affect the efficiency of the board's turning ability.

Snowboard Construction

A snowboard is constructed of many materials sandwiched together. The board deck, shell, core, and base are surrounded by the sidewalls and edges. The different types of construction vary considerably from one manufacturer to the next, and new combinations are still being developed.

The Deck

The deck or top of the board and the sidewalls are often made of ABS (a durable, strong, and scratch-resistant plastic). It's also an easy surface upon which snowboard manufacturers can apply screened graphics.

The Core

The core of the board is wood or polyurethane. A wood-laminate core comes in two configurations: vertical and horizontal. Vertical construction is very desirable. The side-by-side arrangement across the board gives the board more vertical rigidity, making it stronger and springier. Horizontal laminates have several drawbacks and are consequently used by few manufacturers. Other materials are often added to wood-core construction to improve the board's characteristics and handling.

Polyurethane cores, or foam cores, are commonly used because of their low cost and durability. Boards made this way are very responsive and cost less than models with wood cores.

The newest type of core construction is the honeycomb. Built of aluminum or other super-light materials, this type of core offers the strength of wood and the lightness of foam.

The Shell and Other Construction Materials

Foam and honeycomb cores are covered with a shell. This shell can be made of several different materials, such as aluminum, fiberglass, carbon fiber graphite, and Kevlar.

Fiberglass is a preferred shell material because of its light weight, high strength, low cost, and manufacturing simplicity. It's produced in three forms: cloth, pre-impregnated, and precured.

Aluminum is stronger and livelier than fiberglass. It also provides better dampening, which reduces the amount of chatter and vibration in the board.

Carbon fiber graphite (CFG) is similar to fiberglass. It's manufactured in cloth form, is very strong, and offers great dampening properties. It has a greater tensile strength (it stretches) than Kevlar, and not much is needed to change the flex of the board.

Kevlar is an aramid fiber that's light and strong and provides good dampening, but it's more expensive than carbon fiber graphite.

Rubber is uséd as a dampening material in some snowboards. All of these core types are suitable for riders from beginner to advanced.

Base Grades

The base of a board is made of polyethylene. This material comes in different grades: extruded polyethylene, sintered polyethylene, and carbon-filled polyethylene. Extruded polyethylene, the cheapest type of base, is melted and pushed through a slot to form a base material. Ultrahigh-molecular-weight (UHMW) material is another type of base-grade polyethylene that can be extruded.

The best way to make a base is by sintering, which is done by taking a piece of extruded polyethylene and grinding it into very fine particles. The powder is then pressed into a cake and heated—sintered. The cake is then sliced to form a solid base that's still porous. Then it's put on the board. The sintered base is very durable. It will absorb and hold wax easily and longer than an extruded base. A board with this type of base will also be considerably faster.

A new type of base is carbon-filled sintered polyethylene material. In most snow, especially under wet conditions, it's faster than a clear base. It's not proven, but this could be because of the carbon's electrical conductivity, which reduces the buildup of static electricity.

The Edge

All high-quality snowboards have metal edges. If you intend to ride at a ski resort, you'll need metal edges on your board.

Some boards have cracked edges. These cracks isolate vibration to eliminate the stiffness of a continuous edge. Some boards have cracked or segmented edges in only the tip or tail.

Snowboards generally have a beveled edge, which helps initiate a turn. Beveled edges are common on freestyle boards.

Snowboard Shape

Nose and Tail Kick

Several features determine a board's performance (figure 2-2). The nose, or front, of any board is turned up; this is called the nose kick. The back, or tail, of the board may also have some kick. Freestyle and freeriding boards have twin-tip nose kicks. This is so you can ride backward, or "fakie." Freecarving and slalom boards have little nose kick, and none at the tail. Slalom boards usually have asymmetrical sidecuts with the tail angled and longer on the rider's heel side, giving the rider the longest edge possible during a turn.

Effective Edge

The amount of edge contact the board has is important. The effective edge runs from the nose kick to the tail kick. Short edge contact is good for turnability, but not for high speeds or carving on hard snow.

Flex and Camber

Flex and camber determine a snowboard's stiffness and maneuverability. For a beginner, a board with an easy flex will soften landings and be easier to turn. A stiff board will accelerate out of a turn much faster and therefore will be better for the advanced rider, racer, or cruiser. Most riders prefer an average flex pattern, which cushions landings and also gives good acceleration.

A board's camber is the amount of bow in it when it's lying flat. Camber controls the amount of pressure distributed along the board's edge. Freestyle riders and beginners will want a board with low camber, while a cruiser or slalom rider will prefer a high camber. A negative camber means that the board is prebent in the opposite direction. This type of board is known as a "rocker."

Sidecut

A board's sides or sidecut determine its shape. The radius, or inward curve of the board's sides, relates directly to the turning radius of the snowboard (figure 2-1). On most snowboards this radius is part of a circle. It's important to know the sidecut radius of the board. This allows you to compare the turning performance of one board to other models that are longer or shorter.

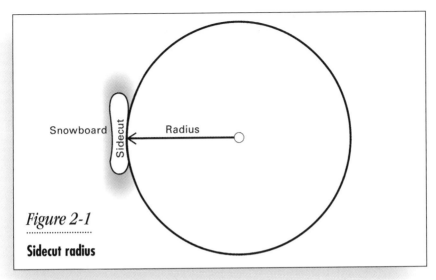

Figure 2-1

Sidecut radius

An extreme sidecut radius gives you more edge control and allows you to do tighter turns. Less of a sidecut radius reduces the amount of holding power on the tip and tail, and therefore is better if you're a beginner; you're less likely to catch your edge.

Several types of sidecuts are used in snowboard construction. The most common is a radial sidecut, which is a section of a circle and is consistent throughout its entire length. The other types—elliptical,

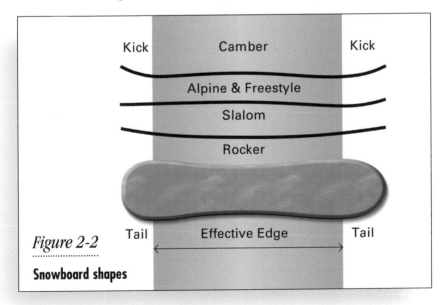

Figure 2-2

Snowboard shapes

quadratic, and progressive—are more commonly used on specialized boards for downhill and slalom racing.

Picking Out Your Snowboard

If you're a beginner, it's important to get a board that will allow you to ride fakie (backward). A freestyle or freeride twin-tipped board will do nicely. Also, check the flex of the board. You want to start out with a board that's soft—that is, with a lot of flex. It's not necessary to go out and buy an expensive board. You can find many good deals on used equipment. Even better, try renting gear for a while before you make a big commitment.

When you're ready to commit to purchasing your own equipment, there are three basic questions to answer before choosing a snowboard. Where are you going to ride? Will you be riding on small hills in your backyard, boarding at a ski resort, heading for the backcountry, or possibly competing in a race or halfpipe event? If you plan to ride at a resort, you'll need a board that has metal edges, strap-on or step-in bindings, and a leash.

If you're not really sure how serious you are about the sport, get a simple freestyle or freeriding board. It won't matter if it's an old model or not; you'll still have fun.

A freeriding board with a soft flex pattern will do nicely for regular riding. Freeride boards are designed for a wide variety of snow conditions. If you intend to ride in a halfpipe, you might want a freestyle board, which has more flex, lower camber, a deeper sidecut, and a more pronounced nose and tail kick. There are several designs available, and the choice is personal.

If you're going to be carving or racing through a slalom course, there are boards specifically designed for this type of riding. Freecarving and slalom boards are long with very stiff flex patterns, high cambers, special sidecuts, and little or no tail kick. Most slalom racers ride asymmetrical boards. The offset sidecut of this board gives it a longer effective edge and makes it easier to turn backside, with less loss of speed. There are also some hybrid freeriding/freecarving boards available; these are great for cruising and carving at resorts.

Backcountry riders want strong, heavy-duty equipment. This might put some stress on your budget, but the high cost of gear will be worth it, especially if your life depends on it. A strong, lightweight board is what you need, and a board constructed of carbon fiber graphite or Kevlar is just that. Plate bindings and hard boots are preferable, but not required. Use equipment that you're familiar with

Figure 2-3

The board should be as wide or wider than the length of your feet

and can trust. Plate bindings aren't bulky and they slide easily into and out of a pack. Hard boots are very warm and can be worn with crampons for difficult climbing on icy slopes. Together, they give excellent control for alpine riding. Look at the equipment that riders you emulate use. They will often help you select the proper equipment.

HOW BIG ARE YOUR FEET?

A board should be as narrow as possible; however, your feet shouldn't extend over its edge (figure 2-3). If your feet are hanging over the edge, you won't be able to turn your board effectively. If the board you like is too narrow, you can't adjust your stance. Manufacturers make boards that come in narrow, medium, and wide. Shop around and you'll find a board that fits you perfectly.

HOW MUCH DO YOU WEIGH?

Young riders clearly need shorter equipment. For most people over one hundred pounds, the question is not one of length but of flex and camber. Your board's length should be determined by where you ride and the kinds of turns you make.

If your riding style demands the use of a 160 cm freeriding board, then your weight will dictate how stiff it should be. Lighter riders need softer boards; heavy riders need stiffer boards. The faster you ride, the stiffer your board should be to compensate for the increased force generated during turns.

A factor closely related to weight is rider height. In general, taller riders should use longer boards in each category, because of their greater leverage.

Manufacturers offer a wide variety of boards in different lengths, and with different flex patterns to match each rider's weight and riding requirements. If you take the time to sort through all the various types, you'll no doubt find the perfect board for your riding style.

It might take you a couple of seasons to pick the best board to suit your riding style. And with the sport developing as fast as it is, you might end up wanting to sell your gear after every season just to keep up with the technology.

Tuning Your Snowboard

I t's important to keep your board tuned all season: It will perform better if you do. Different styles of riding require different tuning techniques. If you're planning to ride in a slalom race, you'll want your edges very sharp. Freestyle riders might want their edges a little dull so they can perform spins without catching an edge.

The air temperature and level of moisture in the snow will determine the type of wax you'll use. Manufacturers are now producing waxes designed specifically for snowboards. These are basically the same waxes used by downhill skiers, but they come in larger cakes to cover the large area of the snowboard.

Stay Tuned

If you don't want to take your board to a professional ski tuner, you'll need the following tools and supplies to tune and repair it by yourself (figure 3-1):

Snowboarding vise clamps (pair)
Wax remover
Rags
P-Tex sticks
Matches
Propane torch and torch lighter

Metal ski scraper
Small fine file
Ski edge file holder
Scotch-based pad
Ski waxes
Wide plastic scraper
Waxing iron
Phillips screwdriver

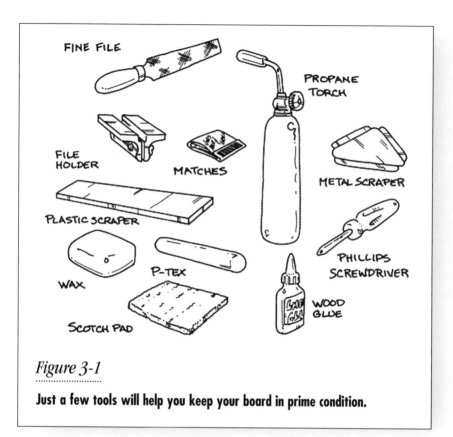

Figure 3-1

Just a few tools will help you keep your board in prime condition.

Tuning

Tuning your own board is good skill to develop. If you have the space and the tools, it can save you money and time—not to mention giving you a much more enjoyable ride.

If you have a workbench, get a pair of snowboarding vise clamps and set them up about 3 feet apart on the top front edge of the bench. These clamps attach to the sides of the board vertically or horizontally and hold it securely in place while you're waxing and tuning the edges.

First, you'll need to clean the old wax off of your board base. Place the board in the vise with the base up. Use some wax remover and a clean rag to remove the old wax from the base of the board.

To sharpen your edges, use a fine file and file holder. The effective edge is all that needs sharpening. Use long, smooth strokes and not too much pressure. You don't want to file metal off, just to sharpen what's there. If your edges have any deep gouges in them or other severe damage, you may need to take your board to a repair shop to have them replaced.

Now choose the wax that best suits the temperature you'll be riding in. Use a waxing iron to melt the wax, then drip it on the board. Starting at the widest part of the nose, drip wax down one-third of the board's length. Smooth out the wax with the iron, leaving a smooth, even coat on the section being waxed. With a wide plastic wax scraper, smoothly scrape the wax toward the tail of the board. Leave the excess wax on the next area you'll work on, adding more if necessary. Repeat this until you reach the widest part of the tail. It isn't necessary to wax the tip or tail of the board. If the wax is bumpy, you can smooth it with a Scotch-based pad.

Base Repair

Snowboarding in early-winter conditions can really be hard on your board. Rocks and trees not yet covered with snow can seriously damage the base of your board. Small cuts probably won't affect your riding, but big gouges should be repaired.

If you have deep cuts in the base of your board, you'll need some P-Tex polyurethane. This is the same material that the snowboard base is made of. It comes in small sticks. If the damage to the base of the board is severe, you may need a couple of sticks.

Clean the base of the board with wax remover before you apply the P-Tex.

P-Tex needs to be lit before it can be dripped into the cuts on the board. Its ignition temperature is high, so a propane torch is needed. Use a torch lighter to light the torch. *Do not use a butane lighter* which could blow up if the torch flame hits it.

Once you have the P-Tex lit, try to keep the flame pointing down. This will keep the carbon (black stuff) out of the P-Tex as it drips into the cuts. Apply sparingly to the cut and let it cool. When it's cool to the touch, use a metal scraper to smooth the excess P-Tex. You can then smooth the entire base with a Scotch-based pad. When the cuts are repaired, you're ready to wax your board.

Binding Check

Check your bindings for loose screws or missing parts prior to each use of the board. Use a Phillips screwdriver to check the screws holding your bindings to the board. If they're loose take them out, apply a small amount of wood glue to each screw, then reinsert and tighten. Losing a binding while on the hill or in the backcountry could turn into a seriously dangerous situation. You should always carry a small multitipped tool (figure 3-2) with you in case your bindings loosen while you're riding, especially in the backcountry.

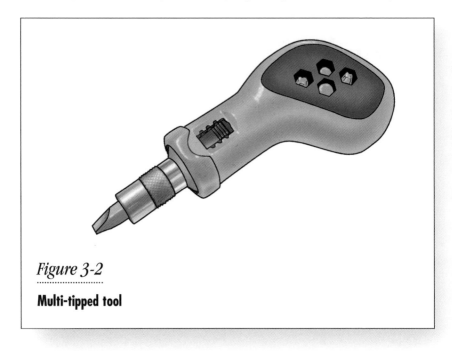

Figure 3-2

Multi-tipped tool

Other Snowboarding Equipment

Boots

After you find the right snowboard, you need to select your boots and bindings (figures 4-1 and 4-2). If you're a beginner, you can start with an inexpensive pair of snowboarding boots. Get them a half size bigger than your street-shoe size so you have good circulation and room for extra socks.

There are many new soft boots on the market today, and they're all pretty good. You'll be wearing them for hours at a time, so pick out a comfortable pair. Check the construction and insulation carefully before making your choice.

Most freestyle and halfpipe riders prefer to wear soft boots because of their flexibility. New step-in systems are very popular and require a soft boot specifically designed for a step-in system.

If you intend to ride in the backcountry or in alpine conditions, you might want to get hard boots. This type of boot will give more support for extreme moves on steep, hard ground. There are many different hard boots available. Look for one that's not too stiff in the upper, or that has an adjustable upper. And don't get slalom or carving boots for backcountry use; they don't have the necessary tread on the bottoms for climbing in snow or on ice.

Bindings

Soft boots need a strap-on or step-in binding. The strap-on binding usually has two or three quick-release buckles that hold the boot onto

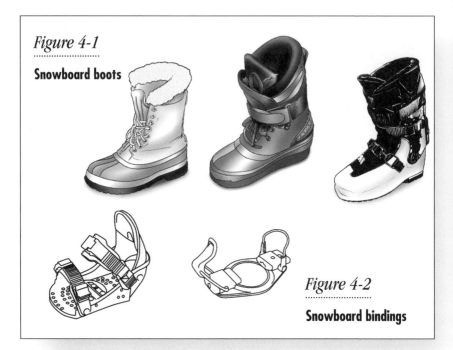

Figure 4-1

Snowboard boots

Figure 4-2

Snowboard bindings

the board. The binding's high back is there to give support while you're turning or doing tricks.

The newest development in snowboard bindings is the step-in model. Step-in bindings have numerous advantages over other types. They're lightweight and very easy to get into and out of. Numerous step-in designs have been developed, and new ones appear every season. Step-in binding technology will only get better in the coming years. These bindings consist of two parts: one attached to the board, the other to the boot. Some boots only work with bindings made by the same manufacturer. If you're interested in a specific binding that's only available with a specific boot, make sure the boot fits first. There are many attachment configurations on the market; look at them all and make your decisions based on cost and your riding style.

To attach the binding to the boot, simply step on the part attached to the board and "click in" to the binding. Various releases are available for getting out of the binding. They usually consist of a simple lever or "switch." Look for a highback step-in binding if you're a pipe rider. The highback will give you rear support and is comparable to a strap-on high top.

Plate bindings are flat bindings with a bail at the front and back. The bails attach to the welt of the boot. They're very easy to get into

and out of, and they're very strong. Plate bindings can be used only with hard boots.

Choosing a binding and boot combination might take some trial and error before you find the best setup for your riding style. One great way to figure out the right combination is to try different boot/binding configurations on rental snowboards. A good rental shop will have various board/boot combinations that you can try before you make a decision about what board you want to buy. Resorts often have "demo" booths that will let you take out different boards and boots for a ride on their mountain.

The Leash

A snowboard leash is a cord that links the board to the rider (figure 4-3). One end of the leash is attached to the front binding (the foot that remains attached to the board while skating); the other is attached to your leg, above the boot. A leash serves to keep the board attached to you should your binding(s) fail. Otherwise your board could come off while you're skating to get on a lift, and go rocketing down the hill like a missile! This is why all ski resorts require you to wear a leash while on their property.

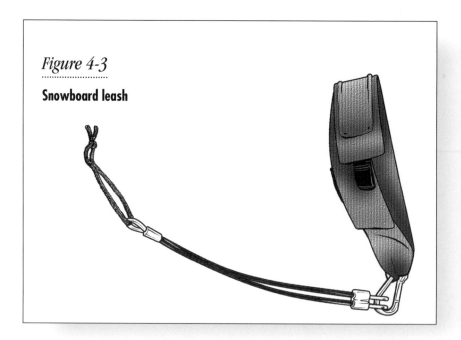

Figure 4-3

Snowboard leash

BASIC ESSENTIALS

Wearing a leash when you're riding in the backcountry is optional. However, it is a good idea to wear one, just in case your bindings fail. You wouldn't want your board cutting loose and flying down some couloir (and possibly into a deep crevasse) while you're riding in a remote location. There are many leashes on the market. Choose one that is strong, simple and doesn't interfere with your riding style. A piece of stretch-resistant cord will do in a pinch. Personally, I like my cable/locking leash. I use it to lock my board to a pole or rack when I'm at a resort.

Clothing

Wearing proper clothing while snowboarding is very important. If you're properly dressed for winter conditions, your snowboarding experience will be not only safer and more comfortable, but also much more enjoyable.

One important lesson we've learned about dressing for winter sports is that it's important to wear layers of clothing (figure 4-4). A lightweight layer next to your skin, a medium layer over that if necessary, and an outer waterproof layer to top it off will offer much more warmth and comfort than one thick layer. By layering garments you can regulate your body heat and avoid overheating and sweating. You don't want to be wet. If you get wet, you *will* be cold.

It's a good idea to avoid wearing fabrics that don't help move or wick moisture away from your skin. Natural cotton fabrics, while very comfortable, will hold moisture. Synthetic fabrics like Capilene, Thermax, Coolmax, and several others are designed to move moisture away from your skin, keeping you relatively dry during intense physical activity. Wear wicking fabrics next to your skin, and layer medium-weight synthetics over them. Garments like fleece vests or bibs are good medium weight options. A warming layer may be necessary in really cold conditions. A goosedown jacket or vest will keep you warm. Your outer layer should be made of water-resistant or waterproof fabric. Consider the range of movement you'll need while riding and pick garments that will give you enough freedom. Some garments are designed with articulated joints that allow maximum freedom of movement. Before you go out boarding, check the weather conditions where you'll be riding and dress accordingly.

If you're a beginner, you might be spending a lot of time resting on your knees and seat. Wear waterproof protection to keep yourself dry. Snow is very abrasive, so stick with longsleeve shirts or jackets until you've gained more experience.

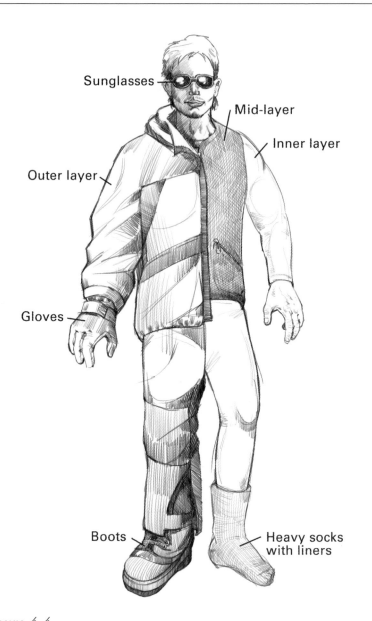

Sunglasses

Mid-layer

Inner layer

Outer layer

Gloves

Boots

Heavy socks
with liners

Figure 4-4

Layer your clothing to stay warm, dry, and comfortable

Helmet

Every rider should consider wearing a helmet. Many serious head injuries could be avoided if more of us did. Snowboarding helmets are light and won't restrict your riding style (figure 4-5). My recommendation: Wear one.

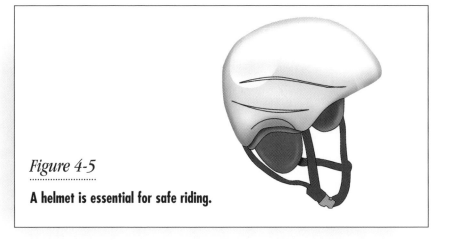

Figure 4-5

A helmet is essential for safe riding.

Eyewear

Always wear eye protection while snowboarding. Ultraviolet rays are extremely damaging to your eyes, and they're intensified by glare reflecting off the snow. Invest in a good pair of sunglasses and goggles.

Get a beefy pair of sunglasses. Don't mess around with lightweight wimpy ones, which will break after only a hard crash or two. You should also use a lanyard to secure your sunglasses to your head or clothing, so you don't lose them if you wipe out.

You need a good pair of goggles, too. Goggles are necessary when conditions are windy or when riding in blowing snow. Get a pair with a large lens that won't restrict your visibility.

Skin Protection

Always wear a sunscreen with a high SPF to protect your skin from harmful solar radiation. Radiation from the sun is the leading cause of skin cancer.

Basic Snowboarding

Stretching

Now that you have the perfect board and all the gear necessary to hit the slopes, you're probably just itching to get into your bindings and shred. Whoa... first let's do a bit of warmup so we don't hurt ourselves.

Well, I'm sure you've heard this one before, but as with most physically demanding sports, it's a good idea to do some stretching exercises before you go out for a hard day of boarding.

Stretching has many benefits for the athlete. It can optimize your learning, practice, and performance of skilled movements. It increases your abilities to relax and to think clearly. Most of all it can reduce the risk of joint sprain, muscle strain, and soreness. A stretching session gives you a chance to relax and to visualize yourself snowboarding effortlessly through the snow.

The following list of stretches is only a recommendation. There are hundreds of stretches you can do. If you feel a stretch is too difficult or painful, don't do it.

Prestretching and Stretching Guidelines

1. Don't stretch immediately before or after eating.

2. Empty your bladder and bowels before you start stretching.

3. Do your stretching on a nonskid surface such as a padded carpet or firm mat, preferably in a quiet area.

4. Remember, when you stretch, don't bounce or force your body into position. Reach slowly and concentrate on relaxing the muscles you're stretching. Release each stretch as carefully as you went into it.

5. Breathing is an important aspect of each stretch; be conscious of it. Accentuate your exhalation as you move deeper into a stretch.

Two Stretches for the Posterior Lower Leg and Achilles Tendon

1. Kneel down on the floor with your hands in front of you. Inhale and shift one foot forward, placing it flat on the floor (figure 5-1). Exhale and lean forward onto your arms. Hold this stretch for a few seconds, then relax.

2. While standing, place both hands on your knees. Keep your heels flat on the floor and parallel (figure 5-2). Exhale, then slowly flex your knees, bringing them as close to the floor as possible. Hold this stretch, then relax.

Photos by John McMullen; Model: Cathy Carlisle-McMullen

Figure 5-1

Stretch your lower leg and Achilles tendon

Back of the Knee

1. Sit on your mat upright with your legs straight in front of you. Keeping one leg straight, bend the other so its heel touches the groin of your extended leg. Exhale, lean forward, and grasp your foot. With your leg still straight, pull on your foot (figure 5-3). Breathe normally as you hold the stretch, then relax.

2. Stand upright in front of an elevated platform like a set of stairs or a chair. Slowly raise one leg and rest it on the platform. Exhale, keeping both legs straight and your hips squared. Extend your upper back and bend forward at the waist. Lower your trunk onto your raised thigh. Hold this stretch, then relax.

3. Sit on the floor with your legs flexed and straddled and heels together. Hold your feet and ankles and pull them as close to your buttocks as possible. Exhale and lean forward from the hips without bending your back. Lower your chest as close to the floor as possible. Hold this stretch, then relax.

Quadriceps

Stand upright with the top of your foot resting on a low stand or chair behind you. Exhale and flex your front knee. Hold this stretch, then relax.

Figure 5-2

This is another good way to stretch your Achilles tendon

Figure 5-3

This maneuver stretches your calf muscles

Buttocks and Hips

1. Lie on your back with your knees flexed and arms out to your sides. Exhale and lower both legs to the floor to one side while keeping your elbows, head, and shoulders flat on the floor (figure 5-4A). Hold this stretch, then relax.

2. Sit on the floor with your legs extended in front of you and your hands resting on the floor behind your hips. Flex one leg across the other and slide your foot toward your buttocks (figure 5-4B). Keep your foot flat on the floor. Reach over your flexed leg with the opposite arm and place your elbow on the outside of the flexed knee. Exhale, look over your shoulder in the direction that you're turning your torso, and pull back on your knee with your elbow. Hold this stretch, then relax.

3. Stand about 4 feet from a wall. Bend one leg, keeping the other leg straight, and rest your hands above your head on the wall (figure 5-4C). Keep your back leg in a straight line with your upper body and your heel down, flat, and parallel to your hips. Exhale and slowly rotate your rear leg out

Snowboarding

sideways from the hip. Hold this stretch, then relax.

4. Kneel on the floor with your legs slightly apart and your toes pointing out behind you. Place your hands flat against your lower back and upper buttocks (figure 5-4D). Exhale and slowly arch your back, pushing your hips out in front of you and contracting your buttocks. Exhale and continue to arch backward. Let your head drop back, open your mouth, and gradually slide your hands toward your heels. Hold this stretch, then relax.

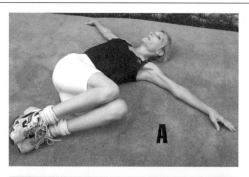

Figure 5-4

These stretches loosen up your buttocks and hips

Warning: Don't do either of these if you have knee or back problems.

1. Lie on your back with your hands to your sides, palms down. Push down; raise your legs up into a squat position until your knees are close to your forehead (figure 5-5A). Slide your hands up to your lower back for support. Hold this stretch, then relax.

2. Kneel down on your mat with your arms reaching out in front of you as far as possible. Lower your chest to the floor (figure 5-5B). Exhale, twist your upper torso slightly, and press down with your palms and forearms on the floor. Hold this stretch, then relax.

This routine will take about twenty minutes if you hold each stretch for thirty seconds. Stretching will not only benefit your snowboarding performance, but will also give you the flexibility to excel in all your activities—not to mention an increased sense of well-being.

Figure 5-5

Stretch out your back and trunk muscles

Eating and Hydration

Eating

Snowboarding requires a lot of energy; your body will burn calories like an oven. It's very important to carry some food with you to eat during the day. I usually take one or two energy bars. These are small enough to be carried in my pocket without being obtrusive.

Water

Drinking water and keeping yourself hydrated is critical to maintaining your energy level. Many resorts provide hydration stations where you can get water while you're on the mountain—without having to go into a lodge or restaurant. This is really handy.

If you expect to be in areas where you won't have access to water, you should carry a water bottle. You might also want to consider carrying a small backpack for food and water. There are some nice packs available that have reservoirs for water and pockets for food and tools. These small packs usually have tubes that run from the water bottle to your mouth, allowing you to drink from the bottle without having to take off the pack—really convenient. If you're boarding in extreme temperatures, get one that's insulated and has a cap on the mouthpiece.

Getting into Your Bindings and onto the Lift

Skating

After stretching, go to a flat area near a beginner's lift and put on your front binding. You can do this while standing. Attach the leash to your front leg afterward. With your front binding on, push yourself around on flat ground to get used to the movement (figure 5-6).

One of the hardest things for the beginning snowboarder to get used to is the awkwardness of moving around on flat ground. Some beginners do fine coming down the hill, but once they take their back foot out of the binding, they find they have no control.

If your board comes flying out from under you with every step on

Figure 5-6

Snowboard skating

flat ground, it's because you're pointing your front foot straight instead of the board straight. The base of your board should be flat on the snow and pointed diagonally. You'll need to have your foot cocked at an angle. This is awkward, but with practice you'll gain control and confidence.

Your rear foot will be out of the binding. Bend your front leg, get low, and push from the toe side of the board. Rise up with each push, and then put your rear foot on the board between the bindings as you slide forward. Balance completely on your front leg. Let the board slide as far as possible, then push again. Practice this until you develop a rhythm, keeping the board moving in a straight line. Next, try skating with your rear foot off the heel side of the board. Using smaller steps, push off and again put your back foot in the center of the deck and slide. Develop a smooth flow from stepping to sliding.

Once you get the two skates down, go to a flat area. Beginning from the toe side, get low and push off. Release and step to the center of the board onto the stomp pad. On freestyle and freeride boards, the stomp pad is usually in the area between the bindings. This is where you'll set your foot whenever you're skating or getting off a lift. Get low again and push off from the heel side of the board, then back to center again. Practice until you find you can push from toe side to heel side alternately without putting your foot on the deck. Although it's difficult, this is a great exercise for balance.

You should practice skating to a stop on an easy slope. Most lifts have an exit slope below the chair as soon as you get to the top. It's important that you are able to control your direction and speed when getting off the chair. There are usually people hanging out at the top of a lift. Practice skating and stepping into the middle of the board, then coming to a controlled stop both heelside and toeside before you get on a lift. It will save you considerable embarrassment and/or injury. When you master skating, you will be ready to get in the lift line and tackle your first run.

First-Day Precautions

Before you get on the lift, I'd like to recommend a couple of things that will make your first day of snowboarding more enjoyable. You'll probably be spending quite a bit of time on the snow, sitting or crashing, so wear waterproof clothing. If you don't have waterproof gloves, you should have an extra pair of regular ones handy. If you can afford a pair of really good snowboarding gloves with wrist supports,

I recommend you get them. When the snow is hardpack or ice, a pair of kneepads will save your knees from injury. Don't let your pride get in the way—you'll probably be on your knees much of the day. Some snowboarding pants even come with removable knee and butt pads built into them. Now you're ready to get on the lift.

Getting onto the Lift

All resort snowboarders have to wear a leash. As I noted in Chapter 4, this cord connects you to your board so you won't lose the board should a binding fail. Make sure your leash is on. All ski areas require them while you're riding the lifts.

Step up to the line with both feet even and your board pointing straight ahead. Look around you to the *outside* of the chair as it approaches. Holding the knee of the leg carrying the board will help you control the board as you lift off the ground. If the chair you're riding doesn't have a footrest, you'll find that sticking your toe under the back of your board will take some of the weight off your other leg and make the ride much more enjoyable (figure 5-7). Now kick back and enjoy the scenery.

Figure 5-7

Resting the board on your toe while riding the lift will make the ride more comfortable

Getting off the Lift

When you reach the top of the lift, get yourself into position to descend from the chair. You'll have to turn to the side to do this. Point the board straight ahead and place your rear foot in its center. When you reach the descent slope, lean forward into the slope and away from anyone else getting off the chair. Use your rear foot in the center of the board to do either a heelside or a toeside turn to stop as soon as you're clear of the chair slope. Imagining that you're actually *in* both of your bindings at this point will help you apply the right amount of pressure *evenly* to your toe- or heelside edge. Ride the board to a good stopping point out of the way of other skiers getting off the lift. This will take some practice, but after a few runs you'll be more comfortable with it. Beware of ice patches when you get off the chair.

After you get off the lift, skate to the top of the run and find a safe spot to put on your back binding. Try to find a spot that's out of the path of the other skiers and snowboarders getting off the lift.

Your First Run

Start out on the beginner's slope. Your first day of snowboarding will set the stage for a long, enjoyable experience if you start slowly, so don't push yourself too hard. If you really want to get the most out of your first day, I highly recommend that you sign up for a lesson with a professional instructor. You'll learn faster, more safely, and with a lot less trauma. You might even save a special relationship with a friend or your spouse by not letting them attempt to teach you. However, if you're a self-starter and determined to teach yourself, here are some suggestions.

The Fall Line

Skate to the top of the run. Sit on your rear and put your back foot into the binding. Your board should be facing across the hill. If you're sitting you'll have to thrust yourself forward and up, then onto your heelside edge. It's easier to stand up when you're facing uphill and on your knees.

Look down the hill for the fall line—the line that an object would naturally take when going down the slope (figure 5-8). For instance, if you take a snowball and roll it down the hill from where you're sitting or standing on the slope, it will roll into the fall line.

36　　　　　　　　　　　B A S I C   E S S E N T I A L S

The first basic maneuver you will need to learn to execute is called the sideslip. Sideslipping will build edge awareness, edge control, stance, and balance.

Stand on the slope with your toe edge in the snow across from the fall line. If you find it hard to stand on the slope, kneel down. Practice going from the kneeling position to a standing position with your toe edge in the snow and your heel edge out of the snow. The proper stance is centered over the board with your knees slightly bent, head and back straight. Your arms will be at your sides. You should be looking straight ahead, not at your feet or the board (figure 5-9).

Once you feel comfortable standing, slowly lower your heel edge toward the snow. This will release the toe edge, and you'll begin sliding in a controlled way down the slope. If you apply more weight to the front of the board, you'll go forward; more weight to the back and you'll sideslip backward. Look for a safe spot about 30 feet downhill from you and slide to it. Lift your heelside edge higher off the snow to stop. This is called the straight sideslip on the toe edge.

Practice the sideslip forward and backward. Connect the two and descend by traversing the slope: Do a straight sideslip across the slope, then a reverse sideslip back to the other side.

Next, try the straight sideslip on your heel edge. Face forward with your toe pointing downhill and your board across the fall line. Slowly lower your toes until the board starts to move sideways down the hill. When you start to move, keep your speed smooth and

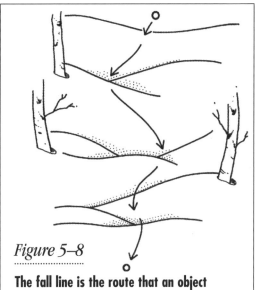

Figure 5-8

The fall line is the route that an object would naturally take when falling or rolling down the slope.

Look forward not down.

Fall line

Figure 5-9

Sideslip stance; look forward, not down.

constant by fine-tuning your edge angle. Keep your eyes on the horizon to improve your balance, and try not to let your board get too flat on the slope. If it does, you'll catch your downhill edge and go over onto your knees. Ouch!

Next, add some directional control by shifting your weight. While in a sideslip, move your weight to the right foot and you'll sideslip to the right. Center your weight onto your front foot to head sideways down the hill again. Then do the same thing, but more to your left. Don't worry about the front or back of the board; just keep practicing until you become comfortable in both directions. Keep your movements smooth and slow. It's a good idea to learn how to ride fakie (backward), which will come in handy later.

Turning

You'll probably find that it is easier to turn your board to the frontside (toe side). This is because you're more inclined to lean forward onto your toeside edge than back onto your heelside edge. Get your body pointed downhill. As you start gaining speed, keep your knees bent, lean forward onto your outside edge, and apply some pressure. Keep your front arm up and your back arm bent into your body (figure 5-10). Bring your front arm over the toeside edge. As the board turns, lift your heels to apply equal pressure to the front and back toeside edges. This will act as a brake. Don't follow the turn too far or you'll spin and end up fakie. After you've stopped, sideslip back to the other side of the run to give it another go.

The backside turn is a bit trickier. Do your frontside turn, and

My best turning tip is to turn when your board is diagonal to the fall line—no sooner, no later. If you try to turn the board when you're across the slope, you'll have a harder time linking the turns. Evenly timed turns initiated diagonal to the slope will give you the ability to control your speed and direction. Once you start linking turns, do three or four at a time, stopping to rest as needed.

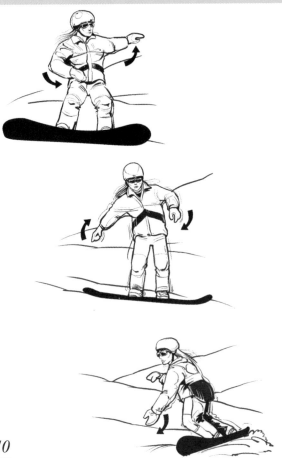

Figure 5-10

Turning techniques: Use your arms and upper body to initiate turns. Keep your knees bent

when your board is pointing diagonally down the slope, flatten out the base and bring your front arm back over the board, as if you were opening a door. Your trailing arm should be bent into your torso. Keep your weight forward and knees bent; apply pressure to your heelside edge by lifting your toes. Push your back foot out in front of you. Continue to ride your heelside edge until you're again traveling diagonally across the slope. To break, follow the turn until you're across the slope and apply pressure evenly to your heels. Practice your heelside turn until you feel comfortable, then try to connect the two—toeside turn to heelside turn. Remember to apply pressure to the edge as you initiate the turn. Get the whole edge into the action, and be aggressive.

Body Position

If you're cruising casually, your upper body will be in a high position. If you're being aggressive, you'll be moving from the high position to a low one to get more pressure onto your edges. Pressure is an important skill to develop.

Choosing a Line

Once you learn to connect your turns, you'll start looking for a line down the slope. One of the greatest aspects of snowboarding is the ability to use the whole run. When you get to the bottom of the run, find a safe spot—one out of traffic—and take off your back binding. You're now ready to skate to the lift.

Sketching, Falling, and Head Plants

Learning how to fall is another important aspect of snowboarding. Since the board is fixed to your boots and there's no release system, you must learn how to handle a crash without getting smacked in the face by your board or breaking your ankles, knees, or wrists.

The best way to prevent this is to be prepared. When you start to sketch (snowboarder lingo for "lose control"), look below you for a landing area. Don't try to use the board as a brake—this could cause an instant face plant into the snow or whatever is below you. Instead, try to roll into the fall, using your leading shoulder.

Keep your arms in front of your chest and your thumbs tucked into your palms (figure 5-11). *Always keep your thumbs tucked into your palms when you fall.* If possible, bring your board over your body and try to land it in such a way that you can get back on top. You might actually have to jump into the fall in order to be in the correct position to recover. This takes quite a bit of practice, and is easier to learn in powder.

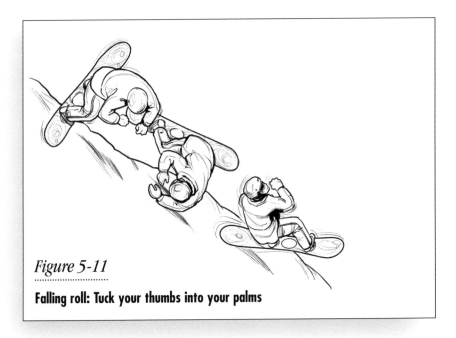

Figure 5-11

Falling roll: Tuck your thumbs into your palms

Intermediate Snowboarding

Three important skills to develop when you reach the intermediate stage are rotary movement, pressure control, and edging. I suggest you take it slowly and learn all the basics before attempting any tricks.

Ice, Crud, and Slush

Practice riding in different conditions. It's easy to get yourself dialed into a few good runs. You have every move wired but you aren't getting any better. If you force yourself to ride in terrain that's different, though, you'll become a well-rounded rider.

Look for areas that other people avoid, like the crud along the sides of the run. On those hot days when the skiers are moaning about the slush, get out there and check it out. Snowboarding in slush is great! Icy hardpack isn't as much fun to ride on, but you should learn how to handle it. You never know when you'll hit a patch of ice. By riding in as many different conditions as possible, you'll force yourself to make the subtle adjustments required for each condition.

The Line

Choosing an interesting line down the hill will also affect your riding. Be creative and select a route that uses the entire run (figure 6-1). Observe all the features of the run and challenge yourself, no matter how easy the run might be.

Look for the outstanding features of the run. Be aware of bumps, jumps, and ledges. A fallen tree can be used for rail slides. Keep your eyes open and look for all the possibilities.

BASIC ESSENTIALS

Figure 6-1

Choose a creative line.

Boarding in the Trees

Boarding through the trees is killer fun, but be careful and don't board alone (figure 6-2). If anything should happen to you, or if your board breaks, you could be in serious trouble. Watch out for branches, both hanging and below the snow. Wear sunglasses or goggles to protect your eyes. Take it easy when boarding through an area you aren't familiar with. If you leave the designated resort run, be sure you're not in an out-of-bounds area.

Tree areas are usually powder snow, which requires pressure and rotary skills. You'll have to use pressure to turn your board and release pressure to keep your board afloat in the deep snow. Rotary is used to turn the board after you have achieved enough lift. You'll use some edge, but not much.

Timing

One of the most elusive skills to learn is timing—that is, the cadence or rhythm between turns. A good way to improve your

Figure 6-2
....

Snowboarding through the trees is fun, but dangerous. Always ride with a partner.

timing is to follow riders who ride well. Study their technique and position, not their style. Ask them to go slow so you can observe closely.

Turning on the Steeps

Jump-turning on a steep bumpy slope is exhausting and difficult. If you don't snowboard regularly, you might want to get in shape for this kind of riding. Drops on a steep slope can be from 3 to more than 6 feet between turns. Most riders prefer using a short board for this kind of riding—one that will easily swing 180 degrees when you jump from a standstill.

Start out on a moderately steep slope. Mental attitude is very important, so get psyched. Don't hold back. Be aggressive (figure 6-3).

As you drop in keep your board pointed slightly downhill. Immediately brake the board slightly by applying quick and firm pressure to your uphill edge. As the edge reaches maximum bite on the slope, you'll feel the force of the turn. Go with it, compressing slightly by bending at the knees, then spring up off the snow, use rotary movements to swing the nose of the board through the fall line, and land the turn downhill. Much of the rotary movement is in your hips. Your upper body should remain upright while your lower body is rotating to the new direction.

This movement is repeated over and over until you reach the bottom of the slope. Always keep your torso, head, and arms facing in the direction of travel. It's best to keep your weight heavily over your front foot, using your back leg and hips to pick up the tail and rotate it through the turn. Resist the urge to lean into the wall, and keep your stance balanced on top of your board at all times.

Tricks

There are many tricks that can be done on a snowboard. Most of these offer you some benefit for normal riding at resorts or in the backcountry.

Spins

The sliding 360-degree turn is fun. You probably have already done many spins while learning how to snowboard, but doing it with control is another skill.

It's easier to spin on a smooth, groomed slope. If you're in powder, you'll need to get into the air to spin. Start by initiating a toeside turn; don't carve too hard. When your board is perpendicular to the slope, lower your heels to flatten it out. Continue to push your back foot out behind you until the tail of your board is pointing down and you're riding fakie. Keep the base of your board flat. Lean back on your heels slightly (do not brake) and push your front foot out. Be careful to keep your weight on your heelside edge until the nose of your board is pointing downhill. Leaning forward too soon will cause you to catch your toeside edge, and the ensuing crash could be painful. The trick is to keep the base flat to the slope without putting too much pressure onto your lower edge.

Figure 6-3

Riding steep bumps requires an aggressive attitude.

BASIC ESSENTIALS

Air

Catching "air" is one of the first tricks that snowboarders want to do (figure 6-4). Getting into the air isn't as hard as landing. If you've never tried it, here are some tips.

Figure 6-4

Catching "big air" in the halfpipe

You can get ready for jumping by practicing a trick called the "Ollie." Get some speed. Move your weight to the back of the board so the tip of the board is coming up off the snow. Push off your back foot and jump up, lifting the board off the snow. Land the board flat. That's it.

Find a small mogul or bump to use as a jump. As you approach the jump, crouch slightly at the knees. Push off as you hit the top. Don't lean backward or too far forward while you're in the air. Keep your knees slightly bent until you're on the ground. They will absorb the force of the landing. Land your board flat; if you need to control your speed, do a turn after you've landed.

Another trick is the "half-cab." This involves catching air while riding fakie and executing a 180-degree spin (figure 6-5). Approach a bump, riding fakie. The trick is to kick off the bump with the tail of your board as it hits the top of the bump and do a 180-degree spin in the air. Use your upper-body momentum to spin your board around, and crouch as you land. Land flat and carve a turn after you land to control your speed. It's important to keep your body centered and straight. This trick takes a lot of practice, so start slowly and be careful. Snowboarding is an aggressive sport, but experience should be built slowly and safely.

After mastering these intermediate air moves, you're ready to advance to the 360-degree air spin. I will describe only the basics of this trick, because it's difficult and shouldn't be attempted without

Figure 6-5

A "half-cab" trick

experience. It's a good idea to practice advanced tricks on a straight jump before attempting them in the halfpipe. You'll need a large mogul or jump to execute this trick, because you need at least 3 feet of air. You should also send a spotter to check the landing-area conditions and make sure there are no trees, stumps, or rocks you might hit.

As you leave the top of the jump or pipe from your crouched position, you must use your upper body to get the spin initiated. Turn your head in the direction you want to spin. Also, drive your elbow in the same direction, pulling the opposite elbow into your chest. Keep your body straight. Be sure to land the transition directly on top of the board, with your weight centered and the board flat. Don't forget to bend your knees before you land. There's not much advice I can give on this one. It's going to take some practice. Wear a helmet.

There are many radical tricks to learn as a snowboarder. I can't describe all of them, or the entire lingo, here. However, if you hang out on the slopes or around the halfpipe you'll meet other snowboarders, and observing them will help you understand how the advanced tricks are practiced and performed. You might want to consider taking lessons from a certified PSIA (Professional Ski Instructors of America) instructor.

Competitive Snowboarding

Snowboarding competitions began soon after the first snowboards were made. The Jem Corporation, maker of the Snurfer board, sponsored the first competitions, held in the northeastern United States.

The usual terrain was a smooth slope. Competitors ripped down this glassy run to see how fast they could get to the finish line. Speed was the objective.

Years later, given the development of the snowboard and its bindings, competition organizers tried to make the competitions fair by forming divisions—slalom, downhill, and freestyle riding.

Later, the halfpipe was developed. This type of competitive riding is similar to skateboard halfpipe competitions. A snowboarding halfpipe—it looks like a section of a pipe that's cut in half—is cut into a slope so that one end is higher than the other. This allows you to gain enough speed to perform tricks off the walls. Halfpipe riding is a dynamic form of the sport of snowboarding. There are many tricks that can be performed in the halfpipe but not when you're freeriding.

It takes a very aggressive personality to be a halfpipe snowboarding competitor. Crashes are not unusual, so it takes a lot of determination to become a good halfpipe rider.

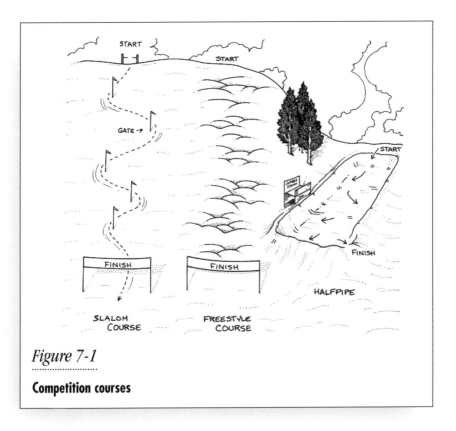

Figure 7-1

Competition courses

Interview

When the first edition of this book was published in 1989, Damian Sanders was one of the best halfpipe riders in the United States. At that time I talked to Damian and found out what it takes to become a great halfpipe rider. His observations are still valid today.

Q: Damian, when did you start snowboarding, and who or what turned you on to the sport?

A: In 1983 my brother Chris started a new company called Avalanche, which manufactures snowboards. He gave me the first board made by Avalanche.

Q: *Did you have any idols as a beginner? Who inspired you the most?*

A: In the early days my idols were skateboarders, people like Cristian Hosoi and Lester Kasai. The snowboarder I emulate is Terry Kidwell; he's better than everyone is. My idols get big air.

Q: *How did you get involved in competitive snowboarding?*

A: When I started competing, there were only a hundred or so competitors; you had a good chance of winning. I've been competing ever since.

Q: *Do you compete in any events besides the halfpipe?*

A: No, I only compete in freestyle competitions.

Q: *Are you interested in any other sports?*

A: Yes. I enjoy skateboarding, surfing, and riding motorcycles.

Q: *What is it that motivates you to be so radical in the pipe or on the slopes?*

A: I get no thrill (adrenaline rush) when my board is on the ground. The higher I get, the more of a rush the sport is.

Q: *What steps do you take when you're learning a new trick?*

A: I go to the halfpipe, I run through the trick many times in my mind. I visualize every move I'm going to make from the time I leave the jump until I land. Then I actually try the trick in the pipe. I try it over and over again until I make it.

Q: *Do you think snowboarding equipment can be improved? If so, what developments do you foresee in the future?*

A: Yes, I have many ideas for the improvement of boots and bindings. Step-in bindings and combination soft boots will be improved in the future.

Q: *When is your next competition? What do you do to prepare yourself for a big event?*

A: The competition season starts early next year. To prepare for a competition I freeride, and then right before the event I practice in the halfpipe.

Q: *What will you do after you stop competing? Will you continue to be involved in the sport?*

A: After I stop competing I want to be more involved with product development. I have a lot of ideas to work on.

Q: *Do you have any advice you would like to give anyone wanting to get into competitive snowboarding?*

A: Yeh, don't rush it. Have fun snowboarding just for fun. If you feel you must compete, prepare yourself for a lot of upset.

A lot of Damian's dreams and predictions have come true!

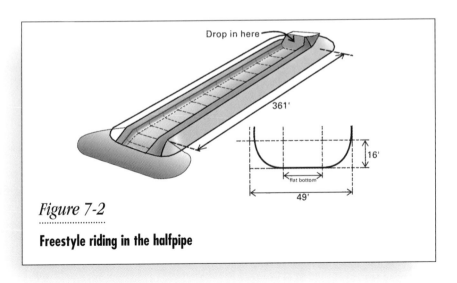

Figure 7-2

Freestyle riding in the halfpipe

Backcountry Snowboarding

S ome of the greatest experiences I have had as a snowboarder are the trips I've taken into the backcountry. While living in Jackson, Wyoming, I had the honor of snowboarding with a lot of great riders and finding some of the most fantastic backcountry runs in the United States. The thrill of climbing beautiful mountains in the Tetons, then boarding down their ridges and couloirs, is one I'll never forget. Backcountry snowboarding requires you to know more than snowboarding; you also need the skills of sports such as backcountry skiing, snowshoeing, hiking, moun- taineering, and ice climbing. If you venture into the mountains to snowboard, you'll need to understand the conditions and respect them.

Avalanche Danger

Avalanche conditions are a serious problem in the backcountry, and the more you know about snow, the safer you'll be. If you intend to board in an avalanche-prone area, you should always board with a group and wear a radio transmitter—a radio that both transmits and receives signals (figure 8-1). If you get caught in an avalanche, your partner(s) will be able to find you faster if you're wearing one. Many ski resorts and backcountry outfitters offer seminars on avalanche awareness and rescue. I suggest you attend one of these workshops if you intend to snowboard in the mountains.

Backcountry Equipment

When traveling into the mountains, you'll need some equipment for snow travel and safety. It's a good idea to carry a good backpack with a small first-aid kit, compass, extra clothing, sunblock, energy bars, a shovel, ice axe, radio transceiver, and water bottle (with thermal protection, if necessary).

The backpack should have enough room to carry your snowboard and gear or be designed to carry the board on the outside of the pack. Snowshoes are good to have if you'll be hiking up deep snow. You may need them for climbing or traversing a slope. Collapsible ski poles aren't essential, but they do come in handy on the flats or while hiking. Also, carry a space blanket and a flashlight or headlamp if you're going to be out after dark.

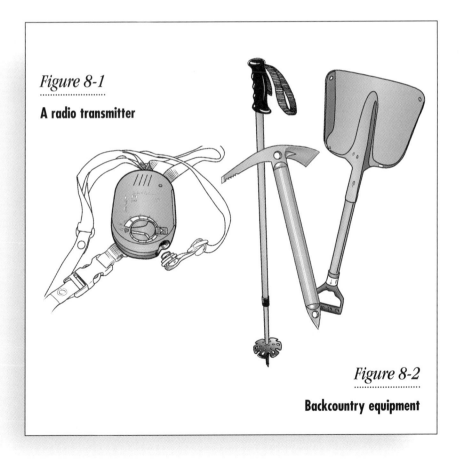

Figure 8-1

A radio transmitter

Figure 8-2

Backcountry equipment

Split Snowboards

If you're interested in getting a specialized snowboard for backcountry skiing and riding, you might want to check out a "split" board.

Voilé made the first production model of a split snowboard, appropriately called the *Split Decision*. This board is actually made up of two boards that can be used as skis (with or without climbing skins) during the approach or snow-climbing section of a backcountry trip. The two boards can be put together to create a stable snowboard platform for the descent. This design is very efficient, especially if you're making a weight-critical trip into the mountains.

Another option, for those who have an old board lying around and are willing to cut it in half: Get a split kit and make your own split board. I've heard that building your own split board isn't too difficult.

Interview

Two of the most experienced veteran backcountry snowboarders in the United States are Jim Zellers and Bonnie Leary (now husband and wife). Their adventures have taken them to Alaska, the Palisades, Patagonia, New Zealand, and many other mountainous areas of the world.

The following is an interview with these explorers.

Q: *When did you start snowboarding?*

Jim: In 1978.

Q: *How about you, Bonnie?*

Bonnie: I started in 1985.

Q: *Why did you stop competing?*

Jim: I stopped competing after the 1988 world championships.

Bonnie: Most competitions were unorganized and unprofessional— i.e., biased toward the sponsor's rider. It was a lot of work for a small return. I enjoy snowboarding more than standing around watching others waiting for my turn.

Q: *What is it that you enjoy most about backcountry snowboarding?*

Bonnie: The backcountry!

Jim: I enjoy the lack of structured rules. The fact that I have to depend on my partners or myself. Everything is open, and I don't have to deal with so many people.

Q: *Do you think backcountry snowboarding is more dangerous than any other form of the sport?*

Bonnie: Not more dangerous, just many more factors to consider. Mountaineering knowledge is required. Help is a long way away.

Jim: In the backcountry I'm a little more conservative because of the distance to help. I push it hard at the ski areas to improve my backcountry performance. In the backcountry I'm usually at 70 percent, so I need to up my 100 percent performance at the ski area to make my 70 percent higher.

Q: *If someone asked you how to prepare for backcountry snowboarding, what would you recommend?*

Jim: To prepare for the backcountry, I suggest some wilderness, snow, or climbing courses. There are a lot of schools around the country to teach the basics of the backcountry. In Lake Tahoe the Alpine Skills Institute has offered the first-ever course combining snowboarding and the backcountry.

Q: *Do you think the sport will develop more? What developments do you foresee?*

Jim: The sport will constantly be developing in the near future. The biggest development will be total acceptance. Others will soon be aware that the snowboard is the ultimate sliding tool with no other function than fun! A generation will grow up and a large diverse group will be riding. Snowboards will change slightly, but the big development will be with boots and bindings. Eventually there will be a step-in system with a flexible boot.

Bonnie: There will always be a backcountry faction. It will never be as big as the resort faction, but I feel as friends introduce more peo-

Snowboarding   **57**

ple into it, they will pick it up. I think crossover sports will develop, like randonée and climbing.

Q: *What are some of the challenges that you look forward to in the future?*

Bonnie: I would like to do a snowboard descent of Mount Aspiring in New Zealand, and some Sierra descents.

Jim: I look forward to really pushing the limits of steep descents and adventure snowboarding. I would like to set a precedent in steep descents and hopefully inspire others to do the real radical stuff. This I'll never do. Specific challenges would be peaks in the Himalayas, Alaska, and in the Canadian Arctic. However, I would spend a lifetime in the Sierras on nameless peaks and chutes, which is what I bet I'll end up doing for the rest of my life.

Q: *How long will you continue to snowboard?*

Bonnie: Always.

Jim: I will continue snowboarding until my grandkids carry me off the hill and they take my board away.

Ethics and Safety

The sport of snowboarding has not always been accepted the way it is now. In fact it's still not allowed at a few ski resorts. All ski areas enforce a skier's responsibility code. If skiers don't comply with this code, they may lose their pass or be asked to leave the area. Snowboarders follow the same rules as skiers.

Skier's Responsibility Code

1. Ski under control and in such a manner that you can stop or avoid other skiers or objects.

Translation:

♦ Ride at your ability level.

♦ Don't attempt jumps that are over your ability level.

♦ Never jump where you're not absolutely certain that the landing area is clear.

♦ Have a friend spot you below a jump.

♦ Make sure your equipment is in good shape, and that it fits.

♦ Safety leashes, metal edges, and supportive boots and bindings are required.

2. When skiing downhill or overtaking another skier, you must avoid the skier below you.

3. You must not stop where you obstruct a trail or are not visible from above.

Translation:

◆ Move out of the way when you get off the lift and when putting on your bindings.

◆ When you stop, always come in on the downhill side of the other skiers.

◆ Do not stop at an intersection, on a blind corner, on the downside of a jump, or under a chairlift.

◆ If you sit down to rest or to fasten your bindings, do so to the side of the trail.

4. When entering a trail or starting downhill, yield to other skiers.

Translation:
 ◆ Check uphill and peripherally when cutting across a run.

5. All skiers shall use devices to help prevent runaway skis.

Translation:
 ◆ Don't even think about getting on a chairlift without a leash.

6. You shall keep off closed trails and posted areas and observe all posted signs.

Follow these rules and maybe someday all ski areas will allow us to enjoy their resort areas.

Some resorts have built halfpipes for freestyle riders. (Crested Butte Ski Resort in Crested Butte, Colorado, is one.) These usually post their rules on the sides of the pipe.

Crested Butte's Halfpipe Rules:

Halfpipe users should make a reasonable visual inspection prior to entering halfpipe and will be held to have assumed the risk in using halfpipe.

BLACK DIAMOND

1. Snowboards only.
2. No inverted aerials.
3. Only two snowboarders allowed in halfpipe at one time.
4. Lift ticket required.
5. Halfpipe closed daily 10:30 A.M. to 12:00 P.M. for ski school classes.

Remember that your actions at a resort reflect on the actions of all snowboarders. If you aren't obeying the rules, it could cause the sport and all its participants to lose the right to use the area.

Glossary

Air: When your snowboard leaves the ground. Many tricks can be performed in the air.

ABS: A strong plastic used for the deck material in snowboard construction.

Aluminum: A lightweight metal commonly used in the construction of snowboards. Stronger than fiberglass, aluminum provides better damping.

Angle: The angle of your feet on the board.

Asymmetrical: This term applies to boards with shifted sidecuts, where the overall shape is designed for one stance, regular or goofy.

Backside: The same as heel side. The side of the halfpipe that's facing your back is referred to as the backside wall.

Bail: The method of attaching a plate binding to the boot. A metal bail on the front attaches to the welt of the boot; a plastic bail in the back is set into the rear welt and clamped on. This grips the boot between the bails.

Base grade: The bottom layer of material on a snowboard.

Bevel: The degree of angle from the base to the edge.

Binding: The mechanism used to connect your boots to the board.

Bogged: When a rider is slowed by deep snow.

Boned: Boned out, or boning, refers to a straight-leg move.

Camber: The amount of arch in the board when you put it flat on the floor.

Cant: The amount of angle that either foot is tilted toward the other.

Carbon fiber graphite: A lightweight material used in the construction of snowboards. It's similar to fiberglass, but stronger. It comes in a cloth form, which is layered into the board.

Carve a turn: The act of turning a board without sliding.

Clogging: When other snowboarders or skiers block a ski run.

Core materials: The material used for the core of the board determines the board's shape and flex pattern.

Cornice: An overhang formed by wind along the edge or top of a snowy ridge.

Couloir: A steep section of snow or ice that forms in a gully on a mountain.

Crampon: A device made for climbing on ice or snow that's constructed of metal and shaped like the sole of a boot, with spikes on the bottom. It's attached to a boot by straps or a step-in binding.

Dampening: A reduction in the chatter and vibration of the snowboard.

Drop: Jumping off a cornice or cliff.

Dual slalom: A slalom race involving two riders racing at the same time.

Edge: The metal edge that runs completely around the base on the bottom of the board.

Effective edge: The length of the edge that's in contact with the snow during a turn.

Extruded base: Polyethylene that's melted and pressed through a form to make the base.

Fakie: When a rider's rear foot is forward to the direction of travel.

Fall line: An imaginary line down the slope. The path a falling object will take.

B A S I C   E S S E N T I A L S

Fiberglass: Epoxy resin and layers of glass-fiber cloth are used to construct this material for many snowboards.

Flex: How easily the board bends.

Frontside: The side of the board that the rider faces. The same as the toe side.

Half-cab: A freeriding maneuver in which you approach a bump fakie, get air, do a 180-degree spin, and land in a regular forward position.

Halfpipe: A section of snow, either natural or man-made, that looks like a pipe cut in half lengthwise.

Hand plant: An aerial move in which you touch the lip of the pipe.

Hardpack: A snow condition where the snow is groomed then packed to leave a very hard surface.

Heel side: The edge of the board under the rider's heel.

Insert: A threaded nut placed in the board so you can mount the bindings without drilling holes.

Invert: An aerial maneuver in which you're upside down and not touching the lip of the pipe—way radical!

Line: The route you choose to take.

Mogul: The crisscross turning patterns of downhill skiers leave a field of bumps on the hill. These bumps are called moguls.

Mounting plate: An aluminum or other reinforced plate in the board to which bindings are screwed directly.

Nose: The widest point at the front end of a snowboard.

Peips: Brand name of a popular radio device worn by skiers in avalanche-prone areas. It enables rescuers to locate and retrieve a buried party quickly.

Polyurethane: Polyurethane, or foam, is commonly used as a core material because of its durability and low cost.

Post holing: Walking in deep snow without snowshoes or skis.

Powder: A large accumulation of dry snow.

PSIA: Professional Ski Instructors of America.

P-Tex: A stick form of polyurethane used to fill the cuts in the base of skis or snowboards.

Rad: Short for radical. Something wild or crazy might be called rad.

Rail slide: A rail is a section of wood, usually a post, positioned on the lip of a halfpipe. A rider will use the rail to perform tricks, such as sliding along the rail.

Raging: Having a good day. Going fast.

Ripped: A perfectly executed maneuver.

Rollout deck: The area of a halfpipe where you finish and exit the pipe.

Run: A prepared area designed for skiing or snowboarding. Each is usually given a name and rating of difficulty.

Shred: To have a great time, or a perfect day!

Sidecut: The difference between the waist width and the nose and tail width. Several types of curves are used in shaping sidecuts: radial, elliptical, quadratic, and progressive.

Sideslip: A basic maneuver performed facing uphill or downhill while the board is flat on the snow and perpendicular to the slope.

Sinter: To grind polyethylene into particles, then heat it and press it together under high pressure. The technique is used to make snowboard bases.

Sketch: When a rider is about to crash.

Slalom: A downhill race. Courses of obstacles—called gates—are positioned down a hill. The rider goes from side to side around the gates. Two identical courses are set side by side, and riders race against each other and against a clock.

Snow cat: An over-snow vehicle used to transport people and equipment to hard-to-reach areas.

Stance: The rider's position on the board. A "regular" stance is left-foot forward on the board. A "goofy" stance is right-foot forward.

Super G: Super giant slalom, wider and faster than standard giant slalom or a slalom race. The gates are also farther apart.

Swing weight: A measure of the tendency of the board to resist rotation (or rotational inertia).

Tail: The widest point at the back of the board.

Tailing arm: The rider's back arm.

Taper angle: The difference between the widths of the nose and tail.

Terrain: Bumps, trees, steeps, groomed, crud, ice, banks, slush, crust, and powder are snowboarding terrains.

Thickness: Most boards have variable thickness—they're thinner at the nose and tail, thicker at the waist. This gives the board a graduated flex. Cheap boards come with a constant thickness.

Toe side: The edge of the board under the toes of the rider.

Tweak: When the board is pulled to the front or pushed to the back of you while you're in the air.

Waist: The narrowest point in the middle of the board.

Width: The distance between your front foot and back foot is your stance width. The term may also refer to the width of the board at its waist.

Wipeout: A crash or hard fall.

Wood laminate: Wood is commonly used as a core material. Wood-laminate cores come in two configurations: vertical and horizontal.

Index

About the Author

John McMullen is an author and illustrator residing in Carbondale, Colorado. He has illustrated *Basic Essentials: Rock Climbing*, *Basic Essentials: Mountain Biking*, and *Climbing the Big Walls*. He is currently the art director of *Climbing* Magazine.

BASIC ✳ ESSENTIALS™

This best-selling series is packed with facts, advice, and tips for the outdoor lover, making it the most valuable "essentials" series on the market today! Whether you are a beginner looking to learn a new skill, or a seasoned veteran needing a handy reference guide, when you want to make the right decisions about equipment, skills and techniques, and have the top names in the business available at your fingertips in an easy-to-use format, look no further than our *Basic Essentials™* series.

Other titles in the series:

Backpacking • Camping • Canoeing • Cooking in the Outdoors
Cross-Country Skiing • Edible Wild Plants and Useful Herbs
Hypothermia • Knots for the Outdoors • Map & Compass
Photography in the Outdoors • Sea Kayaking • Sit On Top Kayaking
Solo Canoeing • Survival • Weather Forecasting
Wilderness First Aid • Women in the Outdoors

To place an order or find out more about this series, contact us at:
The Globe Pequot Press
P.O. Box 480 • Guilford, CT 06437 • 800–243–0495